A Kid's Guide to Drawing America™

How to Draw
New York's
Sights and Symbols

Eric Fein

The Rosen Publishing Group's
PowerKids Press™
New York

Published in 2002 by The Rosen Publishing Group, Inc.
29 East 21st Street, New York, NY 10010

First Edition

Editors: Jannell Khu, Jennifer Landau
Book Design: Kim Sonsky
Layout Design: Nick Sciacca and Colin Dizengoff

Illustration Credits: Jamie Grecco except pp. 2, 19, 29 by Emily Muschinske.
Photo Credits: p. 7 © Yann Arthus-Betrand/CORBIS; pp. 8–9 © Smithsonian American Art Museum, Washington, D.C./Art Resource, New York; pp. 12, 14 © One Mile Up, Incorporated; p. 16 © Bill Ross/CORBIS; p. 18 © Robert Estall/CORBIS; p. 20 © Gary W. Carter/CORBIS; p. 22 © Charles E. Rotkin/CORBIS; p. 24 © John & Dallas Heaton/CORBIS; p. 26, 28 © Lee Snider; Lee Snider/CORBIS.

    Fein, Eric
       How to draw New York's sights and symbols /Eric Fein.
       p. cm. — (A kid's guide to drawing America)
    Includes index.
    Summary: This book explains how to draw some of New York's sights and symbols, including the state seal, the official flower, and the Statue of Liberty.
    ISBN 0-8239-6088-9
    1. Emblems, State—New York—Juvenile literature 2. New York—In art—Juvenile literature
3. Drawing—Technique—Juvenile literature   [1. Emblems, State—New York 2. New York
3. Drawing—Technique] I. Title II. Series
    2002
    743'.8'99747—dc21

Manufactured in the United States of America

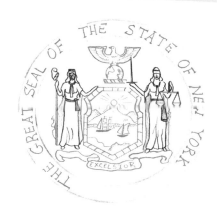

CONTENTS

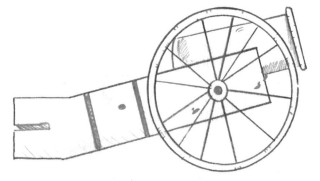

Let's Draw New York

New York State is a world leader in the arts, agriculture, and business. There are about 1,300 museums and galleries, 64 performing arts centers, and 230 theaters in the state. New York also has about 39,000 farms. Dairy farming is big business in New York. You can find dairy farms in the Hudson, the Street Lawrence, and the Mohawk Valleys. New York ranks second in the country in apple production. Exciting sights in New York include Niagara Falls, the Empire State Building, and the Baseball Hall of Fame in Cooperstown.

New York's most famous city is New York City. It is called the city that never sleeps because of all the activity that goes on there. New York City is home to Central Park, skyscrapers, and the United Nations, which is an international organization of countries devoted to world peace. Most major book and magazine publishers have offices in New York City, as do television and radio stations. Financial companies also call the city home.

This book will give you a chance to draw some

of New York's sights and symbols. In each chapter, you will find step-by-step instructions explaining how to draw that chapter's subject. There are several steps for each drawing. To keep things clear, each new step is shown in red. The drawing shapes and terms below can help you, too.

You will need the following supplies to draw New York's sights and symbols:

- A sketch pad
- An eraser
- A number 2 pencil
- A pencil sharpener

These are some of the shapes and drawing terms you need to know to draw New York's sights and symbols:

3-D box

Shading

Almond shape

Squiggle

Horizontal line

Triangle

Oval

Vertical line

Rectangle

Wavy line

The Empire State

New York was first settled by the Dutch in 1624. In 1664, King Charles II of England took control of the region. He gave it to his brother James, duke of York and Albany in England. The cities of New York and Albany are named for him.

The state got its nickname, the Empire State, when George Washington predicted it would be the center of a new empire. From 1785 to 1790, the first U.S. Congress held its meetings in New York City. New York became the nation's eleventh state on July 26, 1788. George Washington's inauguration as the nation's first president took place in New York City on April 30, 1789.

More than 18 million people live in New York, making it the third-most-populated state in the country. New York City is the most populated city in the state. More than 7 million people live there. Albany is New York's capital.

New York City's Empire State Building is 1,455 feet (443 m) tall. Completed in 1931, it was the world's tallest building until 1972.

Artist in New York

William H. Johnson, an African American painter born in 1901, grew up in the small, rural town of Florence, South Carolina. As a young boy, he learned to draw by copying the *Mutt and Jeff* cartoons from newspapers. At the age of 17, Johnson moved to New York City. Intending to become a cartoonist, he was accepted at the National Academy of Design. In 1926, Johnson moved to Europe to study fine art. He lived in Paris, France, in a studio once owned by American portrait artist James McNeill Whistler. In Europe Johnson fell in love with Holcha Krake, a textile artist from Denmark. He traveled back to South Carolina to inform his family that he planned to marry her.

William H. Johnson painted this self-portrait between 1921 and 1926.

Donkey With Plow, Man Shelling Corn shows William H. Johnson's memories of the South.

During the visit, Johnson painted portraits of his friends and relatives. Until that time, artists rarely painted formal portraits of African American people. Johnson and his wife moved to New York City in 1938. He got a job with a government art project in Harlem, then the largest African American community in America. Working in Harlem placed Johnson in the middle of the excitement and the energy of African American culture. He changed his style of painting to portray this new life. Johnson's two-dimensional folk art reflected his rural, southern background and his urban life in Harlem. Johnson's wife, Holcha, died in 1944. He continued to paint until 1947, when he was hospitalized for an illness. He lived for another 23 years, but he never painted again.

Harlem Street, painted between 1939 and 1941, measures 18½" x 24⅛" (47 x 61 cm). It was painted in tempera and pencil on paper.

Map of New York

Map of the Continental United States

New York is bordered by five states, one country, two lakes, and an ocean. To the north of New York are two Canadian provinces, Ontario and Quebec. Lake Ontario and Lake Erie are northwest and west of the state. To the southwest is Pennsylvania. New Jersey lies to the south. To the east are Vermont, Massachusetts, and Connecticut. The Atlantic Ocean lies to the southeast.

New York's four mountain ranges are the Adirondack, the Catskill, the Shawagunk, and the Taconic. The largest river in New York is the Hudson, which is more than 300 miles (483 km) long. It runs from the Adirondacks down into New York City, where it empties into the Atlantic Ocean.

1

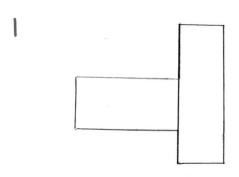

Start by drawing two rectangles.

2

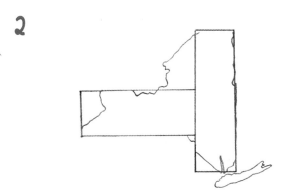

Using the rectangles as guides, draw the shape of New York.

3

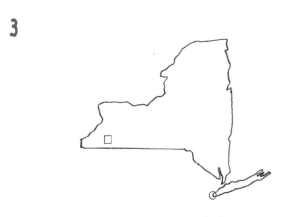

Erase extra lines. Draw a circle for New York City and a square for Allegheny State Park.

4

Draw in the Hudson River, and add upside-down V's for the Catskill Mountains.

5

To finish your map, draw a star to mark Albany, the capital of New York.

6

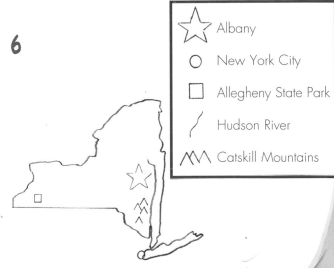

Erase extra lines in the star. Draw a key in the upper right corner to mark New York's points of interest.

The State Seal

New York's state seal is the state's coat of arms in a circle with the words "The Great Seal of the State of New York" written around its border. There were five different versions of the state seal between 1777 and 1882. The one approved in 1882 is still used today. The coat of arms is made up of two female figures holding a shield. The female figures are goddesses. The one on the left is the goddess Liberty, who stands for freedom. On the right is the goddess Justice. Lady Justice stands for equal treatment for everyone under the law. The state's motto, *Excelsior*, which means "ever upward," is on a silver ribbon at the base of the shield.

The picture on the shield is of the sun rising over the cliffs near West Point. Below the sun, ships sail on the Hudson River. On top of the shield sits a globe on which an eagle is perched.

The globe represents the Western Hemisphere, and the eagle represents the United States.

1

Start by drawing two large circles for the seal background. Add two ovals for the goddesses' heads.

2

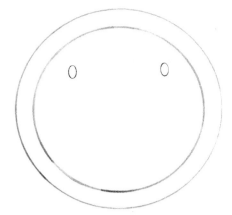

Draw four, four-sided shapes as shown to outline the goddesses' bodies.

3

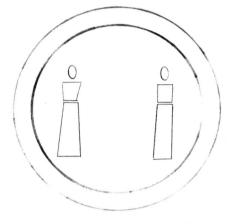

Draw clothing and shoes as shown. Add the goddesses' arms and necks.

4

Erase extra lines. Draw a pole with a cap on top of it in Liberty's hand. Draw a sword, a scale, and a sash for Justice.

5

Draw a face and hair on each goddess. Justice, on the right, is wearing a blindfold.

6

Add the words "THE GREAT SEAL OF THE STATE OF NEW YORK." Add a ribbon at the bottom with the word "EXCELSIOR." To learn how to draw the details of the shield, refer to the New York state flag drawing instructions on page 15.

The State Flag

The modern version of New York's state flag is based on New York's Revolutionary War flag. This version of the flag became the state's official state flag in 1901. As does the state seal, the flag uses the state's coat of arms as its main image. On the coat of arms, the goddess Liberty is holding a pole topped with a liberty cap, which is also called a Phrygian cap. In ancient Rome, a freed slave was given a Phrygian cap to symbolize his or her freedom. The goddess Justice is blindfolded, because she sees no difference between people and treats everyone fairly.

1

Draw a large rectangle for the flag's field and a small rectangle in the center for the shield. Add a circle for the globe.

Draw in the shape of the eagle. Add a circle in the shield for the sun. Draw a shoreline at the front of the shield using wavy lines.

2

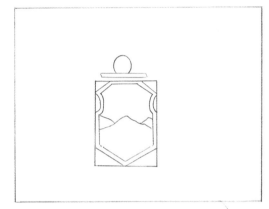

5

Using the rectangle as a guide, draw the shield in the center and the mountains inside the shield. Add a thin rectangle underneath the globe.

Erase extra lines. Add rectangles and triangles for the ships in the center. Add wavy lines for water behind the ships.

3

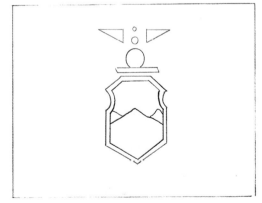

6

Erase extra lines. Add two circles for the eagle's body and two triangles for its wings.

Erase extra lines. To learn how to draw the goddesses on the flag, refer to the New York state seal drawing instructions on page 13.

The Rose

New York was one of the first states to pick a state flower. In 1890, schoolchildren voted for the flower that they wanted to represent New York. There were two choices for state flower, the goldenrod and the rose. The rose won. In 1891, there  was another vote. The rose won again, with 294,816 votes to the goldenrod's 206,402 votes. The rose wasn't made the official state flower until April 20, 1955.

Roses come in many different colors, including red, orange, yellow, pink, and white. Roses can be from 0.5 to 7 inches (1–18 cm) wide. Most wild roses usually have five petals and sharp thorns. Cultivated roses often have multiple sets of petals. Roses are fragrant. The fruits of roses are called rose hips and are a good source of vitamin C.

1

Draw a circle for the center of the rose. Add curved shapes around the center as shown.

2

Add four rounded V shapes for petals.

3

Add eight more petal shapes as shown.

4

Now add another layer of petals.

5

Erase extra lines. Add a stem and leaves.

6

Add shading and detail to your rose.

The Sugar Maple

The sugar maple (*Acer saccharum*) was named New York's official state tree in 1956. Sugar maples have short trunks and many branches covered with leaves. This arrangement of branches and

leaves is called the crown. The sugar maple usually grows to be from 60 to 75 feet (18–23 m) tall. The bark of a sugar maple is dark brown and grooved.

In the fall, the maple's five-pointed leaves change color. They turn bright reds, oranges, and yellows. Sugar maple trees have liquid inside them called sap. Sap begins to flow when the temperature rises above the freezing mark. Maple syrup makers use special tools to drill into the trunk of the maples to get the sap. The sap is then made into maple syrup.

18

1

Begin by drawing a tall trunk that comes to a point. You can use wiggly lines so that the trunk has the look of bark.

2

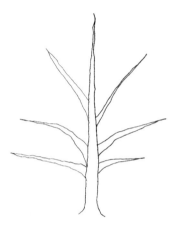

Now add six large branches. They come out of the trunk like pointy fingers.

3

Add thinner branches by drawing wiggly lines.

4

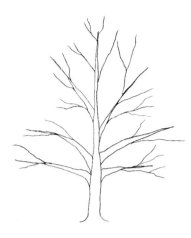

Add even smaller branches to the tree.

5

Now draw the outline of the leafy top of the tree around all of the branches.

6

Shade the trunk of the tree using long, dark lines. Begin filling in the leaves. You can create the leaves by using a squiggly line. Let your hand shake as you are drawing. Make some areas darker to create shadows.

The Eastern Bluebird

The eastern bluebird (*Sialia sialis*) was named New York's official state bird in 1970.

Bluebirds like to live in fields, meadows, and areas with trees. Bluebirds build their nests in dead or rotting trees and on wooden fence posts. They even use nest boxes put up by people. Eastern bluebirds make their nests out of dry grasses, twigs, weed stems, bark, and pine needles.

Male eastern bluebirds look different from female eastern bluebirds. The heads, tails, backs, and wings of the males are bright blue. Their sides, flanks, and throats are chestnut red and their bellies are white. The females have gray-blue heads, dull brown backs, and blue tails and wings.

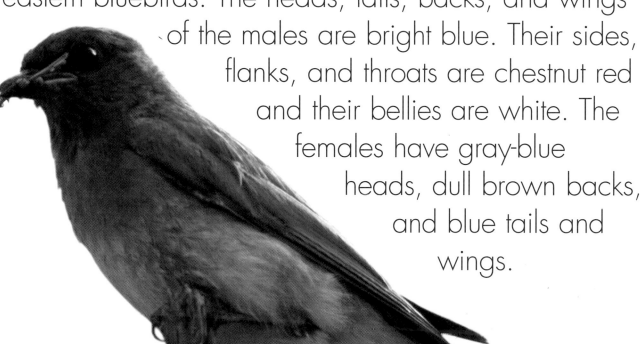

1

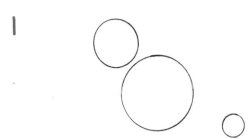

Start by drawing three circles for the rough shape of the eastern bluebird.

2

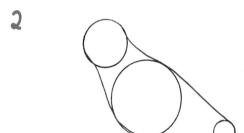

Connect your circles to form the shape of the bird's body.

3

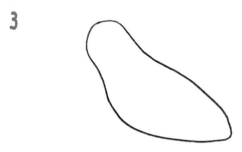

Erase extra lines and smudges.

4

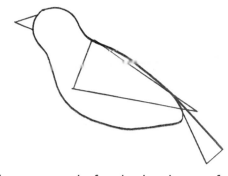

Add one triangle for the beak, one for the tail, and one for the wing.

5

Erase extra lines. Round out the shape of the bird's wing. Draw the legs, the feet, and an eye.

6

Add shading and detail to your bluebird. You can also smudge your lines to make the shading look more natural.

The Statue of Liberty

The Statue of Liberty stands on Liberty Island in New York Harbor. Its full name is Liberty Enlightening the World. It was a gift from France to America to celebrate the friendship between the United States and France.

The Statue of Liberty is one of the largest statues in the world. It measures 151 feet (46 m) and 1 inch (2.5 cm) from the feet to the top of the torch. There are 354 steps to climb to reach the crown and 192 steps to reach the top of the pedestal. The statue was designed by the French sculptor Frédéric-Auguste Bartholdi, and work began on it in 1875. The statue was dedicated on October 28, 1886, by U.S. president Grover Cleveland.

1

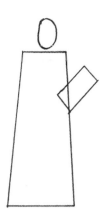

Draw an oval for the statue's head. Add the four-sided shape shown for her body. Add a rectangle for the book she holds.

2

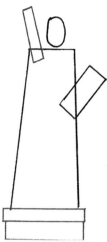

Form two rectangles for the statue's pedestal. Add another rectangle for her right arm.

3

Draw the shape of the statue's arm and hand. Add a rectangle and the flame shape for the torch she carries.

4

Erase extra lines. Draw the statue's left hand and her robe.

5

Erase extra lines. Draw the statue's crown as shown. Add details to her face.

6

Add shading and detail to your picture, and you're done.

Niagara Falls

Niagara Falls is located on the Niagara River, between New York and Ontario, Canada. Niagara Falls actually consists of two waterfalls. The American Falls is on the United States's side of the river and is 176 feet (54 m) high and 1,060 feet (323 m) across. The Canadian side of the falls is called the Horseshoe Falls. It is 167 feet (51 m) high and 2,200 feet (670.5 m) across.

Niagara Falls was created about 12,000 years ago, when melting ice from large glaciers ran into Lake Erie, causing it to overflow. This overflow created the Niagara River. The Niagara River ran over a high cliff. After many years, the river cut through the cliff, creating Niagara Falls.

Start by forming two slanted rectangles for the viewing area.

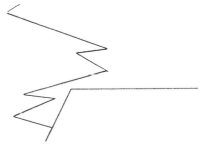

Erase extra lines. Add slanted lines for the shape of the falls.

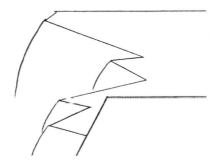

Add curved lines for the falling water. Add a line at the top and at the side for the far edge of the falls.

Add shrubs using little M shapes.

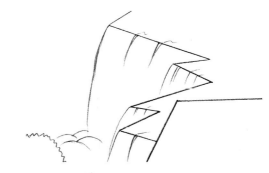

Erase extra lines. Add small half circles for the bottom of the falls. Add more lines for the water.

Add shading and detail. Great job!

Fort Ticonderoga

Fort Ticonderoga, located on the western shore of Lake Champlain, was built by the French in 1755. They called it Fort Carillon. During the French and Indian War (1754–1763), the British captured the fort and renamed it Ticonderoga. *Ticonderoga* means "land between two waters" in the Iroquois language.

During the American Revolution (1775–1783), the British fort held weapons that the colonists needed. In 1775, patriot Ethan Allen and his men captured the fort. The fort's weapons were sent to Boston to be used against the British forces. The British retook the fort in 1777, and then abandoned it in 1780. In 1790, New York took control of what was left of the fort. In 1908, the fort was restored to its former glory. Since then it has been run as a museum.

1

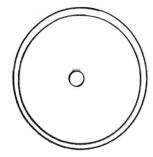

Start by drawing three circles for the wheel.

2

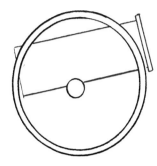

Add two rectangles for the cannon.

3

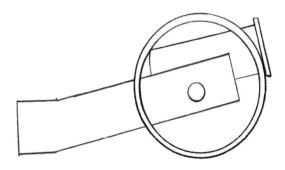

Add the shape shown to form the cannon's support. Erase extra lines.

4

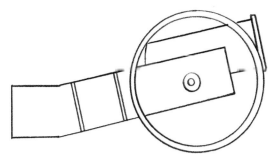

Draw another circle in the center of the wheel. Add two thin rectangles on the cannon's brace.

5

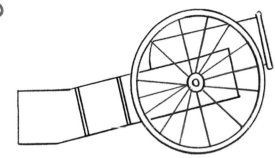

Erase extra lines. Add 14 lines for the spokes in the wheel.

6

Add detail to your cannon, and you're done.

New York State Facts

Statehood	July 26, 1788, 11th state
Area	47,224 square miles (122,309.5 square km)
Population	18,196,600
Capital	Albany, population, 100,000
Most Populated City	New York City, population, 7,322,600
Industries	Printing and publishing, scientific instruments, electrical equipment, machinery, chemical products, tourism
Agriculture	Apples, dairy products, poultry and eggs, nursery stock, cherries, cabbage, and corn
Animal	Beaver
Song	"I Love New York"
Bird	Eastern bluebird
Flower	Rose
Fish	Trout
Tree	Sugar maple
Gemstone	Garnet
Insect	Ladybug
Shell	Bay scallop
Fruit	Apple
Motto	*Excelsior*, "Ever Upward"
Nickname	The Empire State

Glossary

agriculture (A-grih-kul-cher) Having to do with farms or farming.

American Revolution (uh-MER-uh-ken reh-vuh-LOO-shun) Battles that soldiers from the colonies fought against England for freedom.

ancient (AYN-chent) Very old; from a long time ago.

coat of arms (KOHT UV ARMZ) A design on and around a shield or on a drawing of a shield.

cultivated (KUL-tih-vayt-ed) Developed, rather than grown wild.

enlightening (en-LY-tuhn-ing) Giving knowledge or wisdom.

flanks (FLANKS) The areas between the lower ribs and the hip on either side of the body.

fragrant (FRAY-grint) Something that smells.

French and Indian War (FRENCH AND IN-dee un WOR) The battles fought between 1754 and 1763 by England, France, and Native American allies for control of North America.

glaciers (GLAY-shurz) Large masses of ice in very cold regions or on the tops of high mountains.

inauguration (ih-naw-gyuh-RAY-shun) The ceremony for swearing in the president of the United States or other elected officials.

international (in-tur-NA-shuh-nul) Having to do with more than one country.

motto (MAH-toh) A short sentence or phrase that says what someone believes or what something stands for.

pedestal (PEH-dehs-tl) A base on which a statue stands.

Phrygian (FRIH-jee-en) Of or related to Phrygia, an ancient extinct area in Indo-Europe.

portray (por-TRAY) Show.

provinces (PRAH-vints-ez) Countries, areas, or places.

steeples (STEE-puhlz) High towers that narrow to a point. Many churches have steeples.

Index

Web Sites

To learn more about the people and places of New York,
check out these Web sites:
www.iloveny.state.ny.us/
www.50states.com/newyork.htm